GOD KNOWS YOUR ADDRESS

Discover how to face hardships, use what is harming you to strengthen you, and rise to forgive, believe and achieve

Samuel A. Kojoglanian, MD, FACC

A Publication of Rock Your Planet, Inc

GOD KNOWS YOUR ADDRESS
By Samuel A. Kojoglanian, MD, FACC

Library of Congress Cataloging-in-Publication Data
Kojoglanian, Samuel A., MD
God Knows Your Address
pp. cm.

Summary: Use whatever is breaking you to strengthen you.
1.Forgive 2. Believe 3. Achieve

2017
ISBN 978-0-9989210-0-6

Published by
Dr. Samuel Kojoglanian
Rock Your Planet, Inc

Cover design by: Paul Kojoglanian
Printed in the United States of America

to

Josh N. Lee

you are called by God
you are a royal priesthood
He calls you a holy nation
& His own special people"

Dedicated to my parents,
who have instilled in me to
shake it off, step up
and build bridges for others.

1/17/2022

I Peter 2:9

ACKNOWLEDGEMENTS

Bruce Bracken, caring, giving, always helping.

Dr. Paul Greasley, willing, loyal, Bezalel - filled with wisdom.

Arpy Kojoglanian, loving & serving God, loving & serving people.

Paul Kojoglanian, skillful, gracious, great cousin, amazing talent.

Tim Loan, trustworthy, a friend who walks alongside.

Mark Williams, encourager, giving keen insight.

III. ACHIEVE

FORGIVE

~1~
Reject

One of the most painful experiences in life is rejection. I was not born in the United States. My family moved to Chattanooga, Tennessee, from an Armenian community in Jerusalem when I was nine years old. The differences between the American kids and me were unmistakable. They wore Levis® jeans and Nike® shoes, and I wore pantaloons and sandals. They had blond hair and blue eyes, and I had black hair and brown eyes. They spoke English, and I spoke Armenian. They ate hot dogs and apple pie, and I ate dolma (stuffed squash) and baklava. They played football, and I played soccer. They belonged, and I was an outcast. I was different. I was what the kids called "the ugly foreigner."

I remember trying to bounce a football on the playground and the kids went ballistic, laughing at me. It was not easy to be different, and to add to the pain, I was reminded of it daily. "Hey ugly, why did you move to America? You don't belong here, boy! You think you're something, you dummy? What did y'all ride to school back where you came from, stinkin' camels?" were some of the "kind" insults hurled at me.

Kids can be mean, merciless and ruthless. I had front row seats to taste bigotry, and it was disgustingly sour. As a defendant, I sat in a court of mockery, and was judged with hatred. I was sentenced with prejudice, and it wounded me like a scorpion's sting.

While on the playground, kids hit me in the face, and bloodied my nose, once so severe that I had to go to the Emergency Room. When I walked down the stairs, a bully would push me and laugh with his buddies as I fell helplessly. I'd be given a warning not to tell because I'd face worse consequences.

At times, the bullying was more than I could endure. The cruelty and rejection led me to come home crying daily, begging my parents to take me back to our Armenian community. At least there everything was familiar and I understood the language. Instead, they taught me powerful lessons: "Son, fight on your knees and pray hard, and sit on your behind and study like mad. God knows your address! He knows where you live. He knows how you feel. Shake it off and step up!"

The decision was mine.

Shake it Off, and Step Up

My parents told me a story. There was once an old mule. One day accidentally he fell into the farmer's well. The farmer said, "Neither the well nor the old mule is worth the effort to save them." He then decided to haul dirt to bury the old mule in the well.

The farmer called his neighbor and together they started to shovel dirt into the well. The old mule was terrified and frantic with fear. But soon one hopeful idea came to his mind, "Every time a shovel of dirt lands on my back, I will shake it off and step up!"

He repeated these words to himself again and again, "Shake it off, and step up!" This way he silenced the panic and encouraged himself. After some time, the mule reached the top of the well and stepped over the well's wall. Although terribly tired, he was still alive.

What seemed to bury him, saved him. That's what my parents taught me when I was in the fourth grade, when a name like "Fresh Off the Boat," (or in my case, a plane) was pinned on my locker.

Something today may have the will to bury you. I challenge you. Use it to save you! Shake it off, and step up!

Dream Big and Go Beyond

My parent's mule story and their heartfelt advice
have always been my close companions.

First: Fight on Your Knees.

Whatever problem you face, pray. Forgive your
offenders. I know doctors have modern tools and
big time medications to dispense. I know lawyers
have fancy words and loopholes to crack. But the
good Lord has the whole universe in His hands.
I was told to tell Him my problems, and ask for
His help to march on, persevere, hold my ground,
stand tall, fight on, endure, trust, and be gracious
to those who hated me.

Second: Sit on Your Butt and Study Hard.

We were immigrants, having come into this great
country with a green card. My dad had always
taught me that we moved to the USA because
it was the second Jer-USA-lem, the second
promised land, the other "milk and honey"
country. He worked endlessly to get his kids
to America so that we could dream big and go
beyond. Though my Mom is an adored teacher,
my Dad had only reached the second grade
due to poverty caused by the atrocious acts of
the Turkish people massacring my Armenian

ancestors. My Dad, who is eloquent in five languages, told me I could become anything, but "anything" required sitting on my butt and studying hard.

Third: Shake it Off, and Step Up!

No matter what comes your way or what trials you face, this is the way to overcome what is attempting to hold you down.

What did I do? I did not fight back; instead, I prayed, took my studies very seriously, and I shook off all the ugly, demeaning, and poisonous words that were intended to hurt me. Quite literally they were meant to destroy me. I was not going to let that happen.

~4~
Fourth Grade Blues

We had school assemblies daily, but the best was saved for the end of the year. I remember sitting as an odd child in a huge auditorium of fourth, fifth, and sixth graders and watching awards being handed out for different accomplishments. The last award was called the "Best All Around Student," handed to the graduate who was most admired by his peers, teachers and community. I said in my heart, "I'm gonna win that award in two years!"

That's a mighty tall order for a kid who does not speak much English or understand the ways of the American culture.

~5~
Fried Brains

Today's socioeconomic culture has completely changed since I was in the fourth grade. No matter what grade, kids are now exposed to an enormous amount of peer pressure, including harmful drugs. One of the most tragic events in the world of medicine is to witness the diabolic deception of drugs that are destroying innocent lives.

Life will show you just about anything, but the path takes a dreadful twist when drugs are involved. We are facing a major crisis in our land: teenagers are not only using marijuana, codeine, cocaine, painkillers, methamphetamines and heroin, but also abusing it, addicted to it, and shackled by it.

Some experts say that the teens are experimenting and they need to find themselves; that they want to reach a place of nirvana, become more creative, and better understand themselves. I disagree. Teens will not find themselves by using drugs; they will lose themselves. They will not be more creative; they will become destructive.

I hear the familiar tone of sirens daily, but the one I heard one night, while in internal medicine residency, right after my years in medical school, was different. In rolled Mike, a 16-year-old teenager with vomit staining his chin and chest. He was at a party earlier that night. A clean kid. A sharp kid. The music was blasting. The walls were shaking. The house was packed with youth, and alcohol quenched their thirst.

That night, methamphetamine, an illicit drug, was being passed around. Mike declined several times, but the pressure to become one of the crowd escalated. His "friends" called him a "sissy!" Telling him that his "dress is real pretty!" After being tagged as a "sissy" Mike could take it no longer. His courage to stand for the right faded. He did what he'd never done before; he took the drug.

In a matter of minutes, he was on the floor, shaking. Some thought he was break dancing and started to cheer him on! "Mike, Mike, Mike, Mike!" But when he started to have a seizure, turned blue and foamed at the mouth, his friends froze. What seemed to be deaf defying decibels of music turned into dreadful silence. 911 Emergency Medical Technicians arrived, while Mike's friends cried in horror and disbelief.

Mike had to have a respirator to help him breathe. An MRI of his head showed that he had suffered a major infarct, dead brain tissue due to cutting off blood supply. Mike may have looked alive, but he wasn't with us. He could not track with his eyes. He would never speak again. He would never get out of bed again. His heart may have been strong, but his brain was lost forever. He was in a vegetative state, not responding to any commands and not responding to the love of his family.

Mike passed away after multiple lung infections, and left behind a crushed family who longed to hear his beautiful voice and feel his strong embrace.

Just Once

When we make a life changing decision, it affects not only us, but our families, our neighbors, our society, our land, and our world. It comes with consequences, good or bad, for today and for tomorrow. One decision can bring joy, smiles and laughter, and another can bring grief, heartache, and brokenness.

Decisions are made every day. We can retreat to our comfort zone of mediocrity. Or we can take a stand, take a risk, and achieve greatness. We can cut ourselves to get a high. Or we can donate blood to give someone else a chance to live. We can serve ourselves. Or we can choose to serve others. We can choose to live. Or we can choose to die. Don't ever let drugs invade your mind, body or soul. It may cause euphoria for a moment, but it can easily introduce you to your eulogy.

Many say, "It's nothing. It's *just once*. Get with it! Get over it!"
If I could talk to Mike that day and get through to him, I'd get it.
I might even get over it.
But I can't.
And neither will you.

Don't ever hesitate to leave a place that threatens your health. Choose your friends wisely. Bad company corrupts good character and gives you an empty future.

Drugged

Why do you think we are facing a national drug crisis today?

There are some who point their fingers at pharmaceutical companies and say, "They told us the drug lasts 12 hours but it only lasts 8 hours, and we had to take more and got addicted." If the marketers knowingly did this, shame on them.

There are some who point their fingers at doctors and say, "The doctor just kept on giving them to me." If the doctor cares more about his pocket than he does for his patients, shame on him.

But what I'd like to bring to your attention is that we all have a choice. Sure, the injured person who desperately needs narcotics to endure an acute painful stage and in follow up is different than the one who no longer has pain but needs the narcotics because he's addicted to them. But we all face decisions from one second to the next, and we all are responsible for our choices. In the end, we become the person our choices made.

How do we overcome this drug problem? I'll tell you.

When I was a kid, I was drug to Sunday morning worship services. I was drug to family reunions and community socials. I was drug by my ears when I was disrespectful to adults. I was drug to my bedroom and spanked when I disobeyed, told a lie, spoke disrespectfully, spoke ill of a teacher. I was drug to the kitchen sink to have my mouth washed out with soap if I uttered a profanity.

Maybe that sounds "old school" to you. But these are the drugs that run in my arteries and veins, and affect my behavior in everything I do, say, or think. These drugs are more potent than crack, cocaine, heroin, and narcotics. If today's kids had that kind of "drug" problem, where they were being "drugged" then we'd have ourselves a "drug" crisis that would fortify our neighborhoods and country with goodness and hope.

My advice?
Get on the right "drug!"

Mouse Room

On my first day of school in America, my fourth-grade teacher asked the class if we brought our lunch to school. Simple enough, if you know what the word *lunch* means. I didn't know. I was desperately looking around to see how the kids were answering. It was either a "Yes" or a "No." But I didn't know. I started to cry, and that delighted just about all the students. That's when some of the kids called me, "Stupid dummy!" It's an awful thing to feel bigotry in your own skin, to be hated for being different and to be treated with insults. I had no intention of harming anyone, yet I was being harmed.

I had come from the Holy Land, where I played marbles with friends on the streets of Via Delarosa. There, I went to school, but never had a school bus. Soldiers with machine guns stared at us as we walked to school. School was rough in the Middle East. We had to learn Armenian, Hebrew, Arabic and English, but the year we were to learn English, we moved to America.

In Jerusalem, I made a mistake once by sneezing inadvertently in class, and the teacher placed me in the "mouse room."

I had been there before for the most minute and insignificant things, but that was life in the Middle East.

The "mouse room" was dark, smelly, and filled with mops. To place fear in students' hearts, teachers told us they killed the mice with the mops as the mice bit us incessantly. Horrible! Scary! Inhumane! I later found out that was the janitor's closet, and there were no mice. When the kids in America were laughing at me, I thought, "I'd rather be in the 'mouse room' than be humiliated by my new 'friends.'"

My parents always had a way to calm me down. "What is your dream, Son?" they'd ask. "To be a heart doctor!" I'd light up. "Then make your dream come true, Son! God knows your address! He knows where you live. He knows how you feel. Shake it off and step up!"

What's your dream? Dreams are not meant to die. Write your dreams down and then live your dreams, one dream at a time!

Welcome to America

Today, bigotry is rampant. Bullying is flourishing. Anger is spewing. Violence is mounting. Hate is rising. When lecturing, I ask my audiences if they've ever been bullied; often 100% of them raise their hands. When I ask them if they are a bully, hardly anyone raises their hands. One way or the other, I think we've all been bullied. And one way of the other, I think we've also played the part of the bully!

As a fourth-grade foreigner, I could not change the ones who bullied me. I had to change myself. It was hard to endure hatred. It was difficult to swallow the pill of discrimination. It was painful to be rejected. It was terrible to be an outsider.

But I fought on my knees. I learned the "foreign" language of English; joined the choir, singing "Twinkle, Twinkle Little Star" and "Supercalifragilisticexpialidocious;" took part in school sports, relays, plays and government; volunteered for a school office; served in the community; visited nursing homes; and sold the most candy bars in school history.

Funny how fast two years roll by. In the sixth-grade elementary graduation, I sat amongst students whom I had grown to love. My parents had taught me that we moved to America not only to live a dream, but one day, to give back. Two years before, I could hardly speak one word of English. Most all the awards were passed out and I didn't receive a single one.

There was one left, "The Best All-Around Student" award.

The principal held the award, while looking straight into my eyes. He called out my name, Samuel Kojoglanian. One of my dreams was fulfilled to a standing ovation. Unreal. Against all odds. Welcome to America!

Yup. God knew my address. All I had to do was sweat, fight on my knees, forgive the haters, sit on my behind and study, shake things off, and step up!

Cooling the Body

There is a word in our vocabulary that brings much anguish. I'm not talking about terrorism, cancer, rape, divorce, or alcoholism; although they are dreadful. I'm talking about a word that elicits shame, guilt, sorrow, grief, bitterness, fury and rage: it is the word *forgiveness*.

Many people who are terribly wronged refuse to forgive. One of these victimized people happened to become one of my patients. Steve, a 50-year-old gentleman, had experienced sudden cardiac arrest on the golf course. Friends had tried CPR till the ambulance crew arrived and shocked his erratic heart rhythm into a normal beat.

When I first met Steve in the ER, he was unconscious, unresponsive to commands, and intubated, having a breathing tube placed down his throat to protect his lungs. His color was ashy and he was on the brink of death, having experienced a massive heart attack.

Our team rushed in, and in a short twenty minutes opened a heart artery that was 100% blocked. By God's grace, and a terrific cardiac catheterization team, we saved his life. Time to celebrate?

No, not really. Steve remained unresponsive, and I did not know the extent of neurological damage to his brain.

Our team used a technique called therapeutic hypothermia, where we cool someone's body to 90 degrees Fahrenheit in hopes of decreasing the inflammation process and damage to the brain and body.

Day after day, I visited my patient, praying and hoping that his eyes would open and I would be able to greet him. To my dismay, well-wishers and family members were few. In talking to some friends, I understood that Steve had been involved in a nasty divorce, having lost much of his dignity, life, and finances.

On the fourth day of his hospitalization, Steve came out of his coma, and by a miracle, when he was being discharged to go home a week later, he had no neurological deficits. The standard medications were given to him and he was asked to see me in the office.

During our office visit, we marveled at the wonder of life. Steve had no risk factors for coronary artery disease. He exercised, never smoked, ate a Mediterranean diet, was not diabetic, and had no family history of coronary artery disease. As I dug deeper, I found out the mild-mannered man harbored deeply suppressed anger in his heart.

It was then I found out that anger is like coal. Coal under intense pressure and a long span of time, becomes a diamond. But in this case, and in countless lives, anger is like coal. Under intense shame, sorrow, hurt, remorse, and rage, it turns into an active volcano of bitterness and depression. It hardens the heart. When the bitterness erupts, it destroys the person.

Steve was raped multiple times as a child by close relatives. He was told to be "a good boy" and not to tell, or they would really harm him. He was outraged that his parents didn't have a clue that this evil was occurring to him. He was also deeply hurt by his ex-wife who ran off with a younger and richer man.

Many patients have no risk factors for heart disease: they don't smoke, they are active, they are slim, they do not have high blood pressure, diabetes or high cholesterol, yet they have heart attacks. Why? I am convinced that anger, bitterness and depression are linked to coronary artery disease.

I find that many of my patients have had episodes in their lives that drove them to anger, bitterness and an unforgiving heart. Not forgiving plays havoc on the heart. It increases one's cortisol level, adrenaline level, heart rate and blood pressure. It leads to depression. It disturbs the digestive system. It accelerates arthritis. It ages someone faster than normal. Chronic anger leads to an inflammatory process, and inflammation is one of the greatest risks for any disease! Anger will ultimately lead to a frail body and a broken heart.

Steve is recovering in more ways than one. He is now seeing that the coals of anger need to be cooled off for the sake of his well-being.

Pay Day

Anger that is repressed and festers turns into bitterness over time. The wounds of injustice can simmer in one's veins until it turns into venom. And the venom consumes that very person. Anger is not bad. It is a normal response to hardships that occur. However, anger that is not forgiven can become the root of misery.

Forgiveness does not mean you agree with the people who hurt you. It does not mean what they did was right. It does not acquit them of their atrocious behavior toward you. It does not erase the memory of the past. It does not mean you are no longer allowed to be angry about the situation when you remember it; and certainly, you are not a bad person if you recall the events. Additionally, forgiveness does not mandate reconciliation with the offenders.

For many, it is a long process to come to grips with the injustice and damage inflicted on them. There can be denial, followed by a realization, shock, feelings of hatred, and shame. When a person says, "I love you," but manipulates, smothers, molests, rapes, belittles, mocks, distains, judges or condemns you, that is not love.

To realize this may takes years. Realizing and grieving are critical steps in the right direction. But above all, taking responsibility for healing is entirely in the hands of the one who was abused.

Love transforms a person. It stimulates creativity. It energizes. It brings freedom. It builds. Adversely, bitterness destroys. Bitterness sucks the freshness out of life. It focuses on getting even. It hurts. It destroys. It shuts down the very person who is trying to live.

Forgiveness frees us from our prison bars. After the perpetrator harms us, he is not the one in jail -- we are, if we refuse to forgive. Usually a person doesn't forgive so he can punish the offender. But the offended only punishes himself, and pushes himself further into his own self-imposed prison.

Here is a reasonable question: If we forgive someone, and then recall the event, does that mean we really didn't forgive them? No. We forgave because that was a *choice* we made. And the frequency of remembering as well as the intensity of anger will both decrease with time.

Forgiveness releases us from a debt. When someone hurts us, a debt is incurred. Justice cries out, "That person owes me!"

Forgiveness does not come naturally. It is often awkward. It even seems absurd and certainly unfair.

Let's do a simple exercise. Put this book down and clasp your hands together. Which thumb is on top? The right thumb or the left thumb? Do it again. Ten out of ten times, the same thumb will be on top. Now do it the opposite way, where the other thumb is on top. Don't you find it awkward and more difficult? Similarly, forgiveness is both awkward and difficult, but it is always a *choice*.

The World of ABC's

If person A were angry at person B because person B was hateful, and did wrongful, inexplicable, horrible things to person A, person A has all the rights to expect person B to apologize to him. To complicate things, person C may be an "innocent bystander" who did not aid person B but did not come to the rescue of person A.

Many times, person B will not confess or even worse, will not feel like he hurt person A. Person C may think they had nothing to with anything. That drives person A crazy! Person A may first experience grief and fear. Then anger and rage. Or even denial as a means of survival. The anger will soon turn into bitterness. And bitterness will eventually turn into depression.

Person A may wish persons B and C to die. But what person A does not realize is that he is holding a bottle of cyanide, wishing persons B and C to die, and person A is drinking the cyanide himself!

Person A can cast small stones at person B and C, but what person A needs to realize that his actions, or words or punishment is doing further damage to himself. No matter what the pain, it's time for Person A to give himself the gift of getting out of a rotten and stinking prison of bitterness.

Life is full of haters. We have two choices. Forgive or fester. Forgiving is the runway to flying free. Festering is the freeway that leads to a traffic jam of depression, pain and isolation. It is a deceptive road, well-traveled, that leads to hopelessness because it is endless.

There are more twists in this world of "ABC's." Person A can also be mad at person D, calling person D "stupid, idiot, fat moron, jerk, dirtbag, lazy, ugly, good for nothing," and other unmentionable names. In the end, you come to find out that person D is really person A. Stop hating yourself, and forgive yourself. You are valuable in God's eyes, and He is willing to call you His child.

Of course, there is a person G. Person G is God, and person A may harbor a hidden rage against Him, because an all-powerful and all-loving God let person A suffer abuse and humiliation. Speak the truth. God can handle your outbursts. God did not want the crime to occur. He was and still is with you, and longs to heal you.

He did not hurt you; people with disturbed, deranged and wicked motives hurt you.

If you are Person A, it's not easy to choose the right way, but it's the best way, and the sure way to gain good physical and emotional health! Forgiveness doesn't come quickly or easily, but it will change your destiny!

~13~
Weight of Water

I want you to participate in a medical experiment that will help shed some light on the matter of forgiveness. Go to the kitchen, get a glass and fill it half way. Yup, I know what you're thinking. You think I'll ask if your glass is half full or half empty.

Nope. I'm going to ask you to hold the glass up at shoulder level, which may be only 4 to 8 ounces. This may sound simple for the first minute, but try to hold it for five minutes or even an hour.

Soon you'll see that an 8-ounce glass feels like a pound, then ten pounds, and then it will become so heavy that you will drop and shatter the glass. This is due to fatigue, building up lactic acid in your muscles that will not be able to support even a small 8-ounce glass!

Imagine if the insult, hurt or the horrible violation were the glass that you hold up. It may be a trivial incident or it may be a life-shattering rape. Either way, you hold it. The incident will grow so heavy that it will fatigue your heart, your soul, your mind, and will suck all the joy out of your life.

If we are wise, we will not hold on to the glass.

Forgiveness does not mean the glass just goes away. It will be picked up here and there and cause us great sorrow, tears, and even anger. Everyone has the right to grieve. And for that moment, we have the choice once more of putting the glass down, keeping the pain no longer, and holding on to the insult no longer.

It's obvious why we don't put the glass down: the offense was too great; the offender will not accept responsibility; the offender does not show remorse; the offender never asked for forgiveness; he did it more than once; he will do it again; he did it knowingly and intentionally; if I forgive him, I'll have to be nice to him; someone must punish him; I don't feel like it.

If the glass, however, is not put down, it is still held. And if it is held, it will infiltrate the very fiber of our soul and eventually destroy us. The perpetrator does not feel the pain we relive over and over. Putting the glass down does not justify the perpetrator; it liberates our soul. Aren't you worth it to experience real healing?

~14~
Sodas and BB Pellets

There once was a man who was a contractor who desperately wanted a lucrative job. He met with the owner of a business firm to submit a construction bid. The owner took the bid and excused himself, asking the contractor to wait in the office.

While the contractor sat, he noted a competing bid on the owner's desk. It was from a company that belonged to his archrival. He hated this man, who had cheated him in the past, and ruined his good name. It took years to rebuild his reputation and once again stand on two feet.

The owner had stepped out of the office. The contractor desperately wanted to see the bottom line of the bid. By knowing this figure, he could outbid his archrival and pay him back for the past wrongs.

But there was one problem. A can of soda sat right on top of the contract, where the final bid price was typed. He reached out to move the can, but was scared the owner would come back. He held back until his blood pressure rose, his heart raced, and sweat fell down his brow.

He recalled all those years of anguish and all those years of hardships.

He could not restrain himself any longer. He lifted the can of soda to see what the bid was, and to his dismay, witnessed hundreds of little BB pellets fall out of the bottom of the can. The owner had purposefully filled the can with pellets after having cut the bottom of the soda can, testing the integrity of the contractor. The contractor, an honest man, was driven by anger. And anger cost him this job. His reputation and integrity were now damaged by his own actions. Which is worse?

Holding on to the past is like lifting a can of soda filled with hundreds of little silver pellets. Once picked up, the pellets fall all over the room, making it impossible to pick up every pellet. Though it may sound heartless or even naïve, it is the simple truth: shake it off, and step up. Keep the can and its pellets no longer. You will be much happier. You will live healthier. You will smile bigger. And you will soar higher.

BELIEVE

In the eighth grade, my Civics teacher, Mrs. Hixson, encouraged me to become a leader for the entire school body. When I hesitated, she encouraged. When I quivered, she supported. When I succeeded, she told me that I made her proud. She touched my heart in a special way. Please do not underestimate the power of words: they can kill and destroy, or they can build and heal. Be a "Mrs. Hixson," healing people with your words.

At McCallie High School, my English teacher, Mr. George, not only loved the subject matter, but he loved us, his students. His classroom was a place of safety for me. A place where classmates were not allowed to mock each other. A place of education, yet a place like home. A place of sharpening the mind, yet a place of peace. Please do not underestimate the power of kindness: the kind person may appear weak in today's societal beliefs, but he has a resilient heart that cares and a tenacious attitude that overcomes all. Be a "Mr. George," giving people a haven to come home to and find peace.

I spent my junior high and high school years in

Chattanooga, TN, where I nurtured my goal of becoming a medical doctor. My family moved to California after my high school graduation.

Moving from Jerusalem to Chattanooga is one thing, but moving from Chattanooga to Los Angeles, CA is insanity! In Tennessee if you don't greet someone, they'll run up to you, hug you, and say, "Now honey, what's wrong?" In California if you look at someone and say, "Hi," you just may get shot. Well, maybe not that bad, but people have their personal space issues in California.

I attended the University of Southern California (USC), and was in my first Biology class as a freshman, where the professor asked, "How many of you want to become a doctor?" There were 500 students in that class and 500 hands went up! The professor proceeded, "Only 30 of you will make it at the end of four years!" Oh, yes, by the way, thanks for the encouraging words, Professor!

Being a premed student is a bit on the stressful side. It is a world of taking one exam after the other. I remember getting my only "C" in my higher education career, and thinking my world was over. It took me many years to figure out that one grade does not make you or break you.

One failure does not define you.
One loss does not finish you.

At the end of three years at USC, I took the Medical College Admissions Test (MCATs), and applied to nine medical schools in California. My GPA was excellent, but one of the professors from whom I'd never taken a course, saw my MCAT scores and said to me, "Son, you don't have what it takes to become a doctor. Maybe you ought to choose something else."

It wasn't long until the letters started coming back to me in the mail. Nine attempts. Nine rejections.

~16~
Aim High

I took the MCATs again, and this time applied to 18 schools across America. If you can't get into 9, try 18! This was a grueling time because my future was unknown. The wait was endless. The negative responses were unbearable. One by one, I received rejection letters, until letter number 17. I was offered an interview at Loma Linda Medical School in California. A chance to redeem myself!

Before you skip this chapter, I'd like to share with you what *not* to say in an interview. The interviewer asked me, "So tell me, what will you do if you don't make it into medical school?" I should have said, "One way or the other, whatever is missing or is wrong, will be corrected; I will learn, strive, persevere, excel and achieve. Even if there are iron bars with all doors shut, I will find the tools and break the bars down, and get in!"

But that's not what I said. I replied, "I guess I'll be a psychologist, I like counseling people." What? What was I thinking? Nerves? Whatever it was, it was the wrong answer! It wasn't me. I was trying to please the interviewer so I wasn't myself. A word of advice: be your best self.

Thank you for being a contestant in the interview process. Game over! Letter 17, rejection, followed by letter 18, rejection.

What do you do with a Psychobiology Bachelor of Science degree as a senior, who has 27 rejections? My world was falling apart.

There was a poster on my bedroom door with a US military aircraft soaring with the phrase "Aim High." I loved that poster because it described my hopes and dreams. In my despair, I ripped the poster and hurled it under my bed because I had nothing to aim high about. I had tried, climbed, studied, sweated, volunteered, achieved the American dream of going to a fine university, and given all I had. And after all that, I had fallen short.

Just Quit

It is said, that the renowned American author, Richard Ford, who had dyslexia, once gave a talk at a bookstore. After the reading, a middle-aged man in the audience stood up asking him, "Mr. Ford, you and I have something in common. Just like you, I have been writing short stories and novels my entire life. You and I are about the same age, from the same background, and we write about the same themes. The only difference is that you have become a celebrated great man of letters, and I, despite decades of effort, have still never been published. This is heartbreaking to me. I have dedicated my life to writing, but with no reward. My spirit has been crushed by all the rejection and disappointment. I wonder if you have any advice for me. But please, sir, whatever you do, don't just dismissively tell me to persevere, because that's the only thing people ever tell me to do, and hearing that only makes things worse."

Richard Ford said in reply, "Sir, I am so sorry for your disappointment. And please believe me, I would never insult you by telling you to simply persevere. I can't even imagine how discouraging that would be for you to hear after all these years of rejection. In fact, I will tell you something else, something that may surprise you. I'm going to tell you that you need to give up. You need to quit writing."

The audience froze. What kind of encouragement was this?

But Richard Ford went on, "I say this to you only because clearly this work is bringing you no pleasure and no satisfaction. Our time on earth is short, and it should be enjoyed. I give you permission to leave this dream behind and go find something else to do with your life. Go find something to do that you love, something that brings you reward and peace. Go see the world, take up new hobbies, spend time with your family and friends, fall in love, relax. But don't write anymore, because it seems to be killing you."

There was a long silence, and then Mr. Ford smiled kindly, and added, almost as an afterthought: "However, I will say this. If you should happen to discover, after a few years away from writing, that there is nothing you have found in the world that takes the place of writing in your life, nothing that elevates you or inspires you or moves you to the same degree that writing did, well, then, sir, I'm terribly afraid you will have no choice but to return to your labors, and to persevere."

The thought of quitting did enter my mind. But that was not an option.

~18~
Go Ahead, Jump

After a good discussion with God and carefully placing my dreams in His able hands, I sought to enter a Master's program in Anatomy at the University of Southern California Medical School. That way, I would still be taking courses with the medical students in the halls of USC Medical School. There were over 40 applicants and the school only had three spots. And wouldn't you know it! I was the fourth one to be picked. Rejected, once again.

In my plight to not give up or give in, I went to one of the Anatomy teachers and spoke to him about taking a couple of courses as a "Special Status Student," a spot given to a student who was not accepted, but could take courses with the medical students without getting credit. The professor told me that was not an everyday opportunity (and one that no longer exists today). I said, "Sir, I will serve this institution with all my heart and soul, and I will do everything to make you proud." To my delight, he said, "I'm going to give you a chance. I'm going let you take anatomy courses with the medical students."

If hell slams shut all the doors of your dreams,

know that there will be at least one window with its latch open. Stand firm, get your ladder, climb, steady yourself, and jump in with all your heart, your might and your soul!

~19~
Never Give Up

Sir Winston Churchill took three years to get through eighth grade because he had trouble learning English. It seems ironic that years later Oxford University asked him to address its commencement exercises.

He arrived with his usual props, which included a cane and a top hat. As Churchill approached the podium, the crowd rose in applause. With unmatched dignity, he settled the crowd and stood confidently before his admirers. Carefully placing his top hat on the podium, Churchill gazed at his eager audience. Authority rang in his voice as he shouted, "Never give up!"

Several seconds passed before he rose to his toes and repeated, "Never give up!" His words thundered in their ears. There was a deafening silence as Churchill reached for his hat, steadied himself with his cane and left the platform. As fast as his commencement address had begun, it was finished.

The next try may bring you great victory. Even if it doesn't, shake off the past, step up, and never quit!

The New Teacher

I excelled in Gross Anatomy and Micro Anatomy, and then applied to the Master's program once again and retook the infamous MCATs.

The Anatomy department at USC accepted me as one of their Master's program students. Though I took courses with the medical students, I was still not a medical student. What separated me from them was 27 rejection letters.

While working on my Master's, I was called into the office of one of the deans. A thousand questions entered my mind as I walked through his office door. What had I done or not done? Was he pleased or not pleased? Was this good news or bad news? Oh Lord, still my heart!

He smiled at me and said, "We've been watching you, and we'd like to ask if you'd be willing to teach our medical students. Your tuition would be paid for."

I wanted to jump out of my skin! How could someone who could not make it into medical school teach medical students? That's like asking someone who is unable to make the football team to coach the team!

You think God knew my address? Yup! Job accepted! Every book possible was opened, reviewed, and memorized. I poured all I had into the medical students' lives, and took this opportunity not only to help them soar, but to soar with them. I was an agent called at a special time and place to help them. Endless hours were spent outside of the classroom to help students who were not able to grasp all the information during regular class. We studied together. We ate together. We laughed together. We grew together.

~21~
Just Joking

In a village far away, people came to see the wise man, and repeatedly complained about the same problem.

One day he told them a joke and everyone roared in laughter. After a couple of minutes, he told them the same joke and only a few of them laughed. When he told the same joke for the third time, no one laughed.

The wise man smiled and said, "You can't laugh at the same joke over and over. So why are you always crying about the same problem over and over?"

There comes a point in your career, in your business, in your marriage, in your relationships, and in your life, where you must stop complaining and start changing, believing, pursuing, recalculating, refining, and becoming the solution instead of part of the problem. No joking!

One in 10,000

I didn't apply to medical school until I had the Master's under my belt. While nearing the end of the Master's program, I reapplied to medical school, this time as an "early applicant," which allows a student to knock on the door of only one school. In my case, that one school was the University of Southern California.

There were about 10,000 students vying to get into this school, but only about 100 would make it. The early process allowed me to be considered before thousands of other applicants.

There are no easy ways to accomplish a task. If you want to build a bridge, a slab of concrete won't do. If you want to become President of the United States of America, a crash course on American history won't get you there.

Desire is one thing and sincere intentions are another, but they are not enough. Intellect is necessary, but it is not enough. Hard work is crucial, but it is not enough. The love for a profession is honorable, but it too is not enough.

There is a variable in the formula that is easy

to overlook. But without this essential variable, the formula is incomplete and the battle is lost. This unsung hero is called *perseverance*, which endures the pain, persists through the storm, insists on fighting through, and resolves to cross the finish line!

When the review of my application came up, the medical school board members evaluated my folder and decided that I should not be accepted on the "early decision" track. This would be my 28th rejection.

Althea, the head of USC minority students, was on the board. I did not know she sat on the board. After school hours, I would go in the minority lounge and spend time with the students, making sure they understood the lessons. At times, we spent hours until everything made sense.

Althea stood up in the board meeting and said, "Excuse me, I don't know what you're looking for. This kid has been with our students for the past three years, he teaches our students, he has received the 'Teacher of the Year Award' at USC two years in a row, and he's family to us all. He has the credentials. He has the heart. He has the dedication. And he has my support. If you don't choose him, who will you choose? In fact, if you don't choose him, maybe I'm on the wrong board."

That day I was unanimously voted into the USC

School of Medicine! Althea later called me and told me what happened in the board meeting. I jumped up and down on the living room coach like I was a 5-year-old child on his way to Disneyland!

I never knew Althea was watching me. I never knew she was on the board. No matter who you are and where you work, work diligently, work wholeheartedly, work with all your heart and all your soul. Even when you think there is no one watching you, there is someone watching you! Even when you think you are lost, God knows your address!

~24~
My Battle Cry

There will be times in your life when nothing makes sense.
There will be hurts in your heart that are excessively immense.
There will be burdens in the journey too heavy to bear.
There will be losses encountered that can lead to despair.

The time for success will come, but it may not be now.
Gaze straight at the goal and set your shoulder to the plow.
Learn from this season of loss and tears.
Victory belongs to the one who perseveres.

© Dr. Sam

25

Soar Like the Eagles

As we'll see in this story, a difficulty may appear to be the problem, but it is actually part of the solution. One day a small gap appeared in a cocoon, through which a butterfly would appear. A boy stopped and watched the butterfly's struggle to get out of the cocoon. The butterfly tried very hard, but the gap remained the same. It seemed that there was no strength left.

The boy decided to help the butterfly. He took a penknife and cut the cocoon. The butterfly immediately got out, but its body was weak and feeble, and its wings barely moved.

The boy continued to watch the butterfly, anxiously hoping that its wings would spread and it would fly.

But the butterfly dragged its weak body and feeble wings. It was unable to fly, because the boy did not realize that the challenge to battle through the narrow gap of the cocoon was necessary so that life-giving fluid would lubricate its wings and enable it to fly.

Don't despise the small gaps that obstruct your

way in life; appreciate them. They may be painful, but they will supply the fuel to lubricate your wings, and give you the strength to mount up like the eagles, and fly!

26

Benzene Rings

Medical school is not for the fainthearted. Information comes at you faster than the speed of light. You must grasp it and get ready for the next lesson.

I'm constantly asked by pre-medical students why they must take courses like Organic Chemistry as a prerequisite to get it into medical school.

"Man, I agree with you!" I say, "because I surely don't see benzene rings or hydrogen bonds when I open up heart arteries!"

Then I continue, "Medicine is a life of sacrifice, and it is not easy. You will be given the privilege to take care of people's lives. These courses like Chemistry and Physics simply vouch that you are willing to give of your time, and spend endless hours to master what seems to be impossible. Willing to go through the rigors of these courses testifies to your devotion for a lifetime of service."

Don't disdain the painful process and the insurmountable climb; use them as the strands that strengthen the realization of your dream.

~27~
Solid Gold

In my third year of medical school, I was out on a church picnic. While playing softball, I was in the outfield, and while chasing the ball, I fell down a small ravine, and couldn't get up. I was thinking, "Man, just get up and get the ball," but I couldn't move my leg.

The ambulance ride was horrible because in my mind, I had to be back in school the next day. The diagnosis was a broken femur. The doctor said I probably had cancer. Surgery was done. Pins were placed in my bones. And five days later, thank God, the biopsy report read, "no malignancy."

One of the doctors told me that I was going to miss school for eight weeks. "But I won't be able to graduate on time!" "Well, there are worse things," he said, and walked out of the room. That was crushing news, delivered in a distasteful manner.

I worked like a mad boy. God knew my address. He knew if I'd graduate on time or not. All I had to do was shake it off, and step up. Physical therapy, walk, rise, go again and again. I acted like I was

Rocky, training for a fight. By God's grace, I went back to school in four weeks!

My schedule totally changed. I was placed at Huntington Memorial Hospital in Pasadena, CA, for a six-week Internal Medicine rotation. This was an opportunity that all medical students coveted; it was so rare that only a handful of students were given the privilege. The only reason it opened for me was because my schedule was shuffled during my four weeks' absence. Good results came out of a bad situation.

Important connections were made while I was there for the six weeks. After I graduated from medical school (on time), I became an intern and resident at Huntington Memorial Hospital, an address I landed in "accidently" for three years.

You can't get pure gold unless it goes through the fire. Impurities come out because of the intense heat. Instead of complaining about the fire, allow the grunge to seep out of you, and strength and character to come forth within you!

ACHIEVE

Galloping Horses

Fourth year medical school is amazing fun. Students can choose electives in a certain field, and pursue their calling. During that year, an obese patient came into the Emergency Room complaining of chest pains. He was a smoker and diabetic. He told me that it was indigestion and I should give him some antacids. I thought it strange because if he could take antacids at home, why did he come to the ER?

You are trained in medicine that "If it gallops, it's likely a horse…don't go chasing a zebra." An EKG is really all I needed for a proper diagnosis. To chase other things would have wasted time and jeopardized his life. The EKG showed he was having a heart attack and his heart muscle was screaming for help!

We rushed him to the cardiac catheterization laboratory, and my attending physician opened a clogged artery within 25 minutes. Our patient no longer had "indigestion." He was pain-free. And we were one happy team!

Don't pursue the zebras in life. Spend your time wisely. Don't let the enemy's voice distract you or throw you off course. If it gallops, look for the horse.

~29~
Next Station

There are two reasons why I love and chose the field of cardiology: you have the honor of prolonging someone's life, and you have the privilege of changing the quality of someone's life. To get to that level, however, I first had to go through an internship and residency in Internal Medicine that lasted three years.

Why can't someone just go into the field of Cardiology and skip Internal Medicine? To understand the "simple" anatomy of the heart, it is important to understand the complexity of the whole body.

There are stations in life that seem unnecessary, unfair, repetitive, ambiguous, and plain exhausting. These stations are pillars that build your life and make your temple stand majestically tall.

You may not be able to understand the stations now. You may not like the place you are in. You may be unsatisfied. You may even feel cheated and shortchanged.

But when you finally receive the privilege of overseeing an assignment, you will handle it with so much care, appreciation and skill that would have been missing without the preparation and extensive training.

~30~
Octopus Pot

After finishing the Internal Medicine program, I was accepted into Kaiser Los Angeles Cardiology Fellowship training for a period of three years. New place. New people. New instructors. New material. Welcome to the world of cardiology!

In my first year of training, we saw a patient who was a 45-year-old female with a massive heart attack. We rushed her to the cardiac catheterization laboratory. She just had a fight with her husband who was coming home late. While yelling and screaming, she clutched her chest and turned pale. When she arrived at our hospital, she was in cardiogenic shock, where her heart pump failed, her blood pressure fell, her heart rate rose, and fluid filled her lungs.

Her EKG showed a massive heart attack in the front part of her heart. We rushed her into our lab, and were surprised to see wide open and clean coronary arteries. We then looked at her heart muscle and saw an amazing picture. The tip of her heart was ballooned outward and was not moving while the rest of the heart moved. Not many in our field knew it at that time, but this presentation started becoming common in literature as

"Takotsubo Cardiomyopathy."

This condition presents as a heart attack with EKG changes that mimic a heart attack, where cardiac enzymes are spilled into the blood stream. But when the patient undergoes angiography, there is no significant coronary artery disease or blockage, but there is a ballooning of the tip of the heart. The syndrome is triggered by a significant emotional stress such as excessive grief during a funeral. The Japanese word takotsubo (taco-sue-bo) means "octopus pot" which resembles the heart muscles shape in this condition.

Thankfully, our patient's heart muscle returned to normal in a matter of three days, and she was released to go home after receiving treatment, medications and counsel regarding her emotions.

No one can tell you not to grieve, not to get angry, not to become too emotionally involved. But I can tell you to take care of your heart. You've only got one. Be kind to yourself. Be kind to your heart.

~31~
One in 70

After I finished my cardiology training, I applied for an interventional cardiology position, where one is trained to open heart arteries, leg and kidney arteries, and even heart valves with balloons and stents.

There were only 70 spots in the United States for one to become an interventional cardiologist. By God's grace, I got one of those spots.

I often remember the face of the professor who told me I don't have what it takes to be a medical doctor. One day, I just might see him on my table, and get to save the one who tried to kill me with his words.

I often recall the faces of the kids who called me an ugly foreigner. I truly hope they are doing well, and have achieved their dreams.

I guess none of them knew my address. I guess they never thought I'd shake it off and step up.

Black Jesus

In my last year of cardiology training, I was leading a hospital team on a quiet Saturday night. We got a call that a man was clutching his chest and unable to breathe in the Emergency Room. We swarmed down the stairs and saw a man in full cardiac arrest. Intravenous medications, shock paddles and clot busters were at our disposal. After working on our patient for 20 minutes, including doing CPR, we brought him back to life.

I was almost done with my training. It had been over 10 years since I had been accepted into medical school. Joy ruled my heart, knowing it had been a long journey, and saving people's lives was well worth it. I headed to the waiting area to speak to the family.

In the hallway stood Althea. I hadn't seen her since leaving medical school and we had not kept in touch. I said, "Althea, what are you doing here?"

She grabbed my hand, and held it tight, saying, "Listen to me, the man's life you just saved – that's my husband!"

I froze in disbelief. How could this be? I hadn't seen her in years.

It just "happened" that I was now a senior fellow in cardiology. It just "happened" that I was on call on this very particular day. It just "happened" that Althea's husband had a heart attack, and came to our hospital out of all the hospitals in Los Angeles. It just "happened" that I led a team that night.

Althea continued, "I knew there was some reason I picked you!"
"You know what?" she asked me.

"What?" I said.

She looked me square in the eye, and said, "You're like black Jesus!"

That day I got the biggest promotion of my life. I went from a white Armenian cardiologist straight to black Jesus!

Yes, God knew my address.
He knew I was at Kaiser Los Angeles.
He knew I was at the peak of my training.
He knew I had hit and broken through many brick walls.

He knew I had climbed insurmountable mountains.
He gave me the perseverance to shake things off and step up.
He orchestrated the whole event.
He placed a certified stamp of approval on my envelope.

~33~
Widow Maker

Recently I saw Ryan, a pleasant 61-year-old gentleman who had just retired. He had seen doctors including a couple of cardiologist for the past four months. His story was classic. He exerted himself and felt chest pain. Bingo! Easy to make a diagnosis and treat the patient properly.

But a stress nuclear exam of the heart had showed no areas missing oxygen. Therefore, Ryan was labeled as a lung patient, and was asked to see a pulmonologist. He was then diagnosed with asthma and given steroid inhalers. He kept exercising, but felt hindered and backed off when he felt the chest pain. He continued to use the inhalers but felt no relief.

After he and his wife asked nurses and checked the internet, they called my office and made an appointment to see me. Ryan told me the day before that he had tried to run and walk a marathon. I listened to his story, did a couple of diagnostic tests, and asked him to go straight to the Emergency Room. I called the cardiac catheterization lab and scheduled an angiogram on the same day.

My patient did not know what to expect, so I drew a picture, letting him know that he'd likely have a 99% blockage in the artery called the "widow maker." I was shocked to hear that he had been in a marathon the day before; he should have been dead, but stood before me as a miracle.

The angiogram was done swiftly, and there it was: a 99% blockage in the most important heart artery. I opened the artery and then shared with Ryan and his family how blessed he was to be alive.

There will be moments in life when you are told a certain thing or given a certain diagnosis. What are you going to do? Don't just sit in the well and allow the dirt to bury you alive. Ask. Seek. Knock. Search. Fight. Cry. Pray. Shake it off and step up. Use whatever is burying you to strengthen you!

~34~
Mending Hearts

Once upon a time two brothers, John and Bob, who lived on adjoining farms, fell into conflict. For 40 years, they shared machinery, traded labor and goods as needed without a problem.

But a small misunderstanding grew into an outrageous conflict, and finally exploded into an exchange of bitter words. And then came silence.

One morning someone knocked on John's door. John answered and faced a man with a carpenter's toolbox. "I'm looking for a few days' work" the carpenter said. "Perhaps you would have a few small jobs here and there. May I help you in any way?"

"Yes," said John. "I do have a job for you. Look across the creek at that farm. That's my neighbor, in fact, it's my younger brother, Bob. Last week there was a meadow between us and he took his bulldozer to the river levee and now there is a creek between us. Well, he may have done this to spite me, but I'll do him one better. See that pile of lumber curing by the barn? I want you to build me a fence - an 8-foot fence - so I won't need to see his place anymore. Cool him down, you know."

The carpenter said, "I think I understand the situation. Show me the nails and the post hole digger and I'll be able to do a job that pleases you."

The carpenter worked hard all that day measuring, sawing, nailing.

About sunset when John returned, the carpenter had just finished his job. Then John's eyes opened wide and his jaw dropped.

There was no fence there at all. It was a bridge; a bridge stretching from one side of the creek to the other! A fine piece of work with handrails and all. And the neighbor, his younger brother Bob? Bob was walking toward John with his arms outstretched.

"John, you are quite a man to build this bridge after all I've said and done!" said Bob.

The two brothers stood at each end of the bridge, and then they met in the middle, hugging one another.

They turned to see the carpenter hoist his toolbox on his shoulder. "No, wait! Stay a few days. I've a lot of other projects for you!" John yelled.

"I'd love to stay on," the carpenter said, "but, I have many more bridges to build."

35

Orphans' Address

During my cardiology career, I left a secure group practice because of the calling in my heart. To be a solo interventional cardiologist in these heated health care conditions is suicidal. So, I told God that I was not a businessman, that I could not go out on my own, that I could not sustain it. You know what He told me, right? Yup, you guessed it, that He knew my address.

Since my departure, I have been able to visit nations like the Argentina, the Philippines, Hong Kong, Myanmar and take care of the indigent as a medical missionary. As the Mender of Hearts, God has given me the abilities to heal the hearts of patients. As the Founder and President of the Beacon of Hearts, a non-profit 501c3 ministry, God has graciously allowed me to be an instrument in His hands as He mends the souls of people.

We have 28 orphans that we care for in Myanmar. When I see these kids, and when I see the indigent, longing for hugs, for love, for care, for a shoulder to cry on, my heart rejoices that I am able in some form to listen, to give, to help, and to love. I do not pity these souls. I love them. Why?

Because God knows their address, and if He cares for the sparrows, I know He cares for these precious souls.

I'm not sure where you are in the journey of life. Crushed? Rejected? Lonely? Heartbroken? Stressed? Spent? Sick? Separated? Divorced? Rich? Famous? Successful? Running the rat race? Did you know the one who wins the rat race, will become the number one rat?

If you find yourself unhappy, I will share with you the secret to life. Instead of serving yourself, serve others. Instead of filling your bag, fill the bag of others. Instead of complaining, become the solution. Instead of dying, live. Shake it all off, step up, build bridges for others and rock your planet!

36

Step Up Anyway

Life is full of haters.
Forgive them anyway.
Life is filled with challenges.
Use them as your runway.

Life is packed with hardships.
Hold on anyway.
Life may hand you the short end of the stick.
Cry if you must, but rise for a new day.

Life will at times sting you.
Endure the battle anyway.
Life may shortchange you.
Meet it head on straight away.

God knows your address.
Don't quit, help others and keep steady.
Shake off the dirt and step up.
Stand strong and walk humbly.

© Dr. Sam